✦

# THE BLESSING

## OF DARK WATER

# THE
# BLESSING OF
# DARK WATER

Elizabeth Lyons

ALICE JAMES BOOKS
*Farmington, Maine*

10 9 8 7 6 5 4 3 2 1

Alice James Books are published by Alice James Poetry Cooperative, Inc.,
an affiliate of the University of Maine at Farmington.

Alice James Books
114 Prescott Street
Farmington, ME 04938
www.alicejamesbooks.org

Library of Congress Cataloging-in-Publication Data

Names: Lyons, Elizabeth, 1981- author.
Title: The blessing of dark water / Elizabeth Lyons.
Description: Farmington, ME : Alice James Books, 2017.
Identifiers: LCCN 2016046097 (print) | LCCN 2017002384 (ebook) | ISBN
9781938584336 (paperback) | ISBN 9781938584435 (eBook)
Subjects: | BISAC: POETRY / American / General.
Classification: LCC PS3612.Y5746 A6 2017 (print) | LCC PS3612.Y5746 (ebook) |
DDC 811/.6--dc23
LC record available at https://lccn.loc.gov/2016046097

Alice James Books gratefully acknowledges support from individual
donors, private foundations, the University of Maine at Farmington, the
National Endowment for the Arts, and the Amazon Literary Partnership.

Cover photograph:
"Listening to the Mind" by Jayoung Yoon

*There seems to be another half to what we do. Sometimes it's a beast or bird, sometimes a man.*

—WALTER ANDERSON

✦

*. . . There is only one thing I want, and that is that you should be completely well.*

—AGNES ANDERSON

# THE BLESSING OF DARK WATER:
# A BEGINNING

## I. ILLNESS: ELIZABETH

I am in a room, labeled difficult.

The meds make my tongue swell. I can't speak.

Another patient, *Sweet on me* (the nurses say), steals *War Music* and a red camisole from my room. He follows me, asks for my address. I feign deafness, avoid him.

No doors lock.

My not-yet-husband knows this is not me. I can only be released to family.

My parents drive through the night. I watch the elevators for them. For a weekend, Walter, my mind. ~~Beast~~.

*I told you we were coming back for you tomorrow. But I could tell from they'd inject you again as soon as we left.*

The next day, we leave the city, the river frozen. I don't take the pills.

I recover.

We don't speak of it.

# I. ILLNESS: WALTER

After seven months at the clinic, Walter agrees.

Used only for the worst, Metrazol injections cause epileptic convulsions so severe they could fracture bones. *A deep explosion in the brain…made them more accessible to their physicians.*

In two months, twenty-five injections. Eighteen convulsions.

By the fall of 1938, the family boards a train and they are home.

Walter clears the underbrush outside the studio with an adze. It is October.

Perhaps he walked the dock and didn't look for his skiff or to the island. Gave the family hope.

## II. WALTER INGLIS ANDERSON

[1903-1965]

An artist from the Gulf Coast, Walter worked in many forms—murals, paintings, sculpture, and drawings. He made his living as a potter, working at Shearwater Pottery, which was founded by his brother Peter.

With the exception of a yearlong hospital stay in his early thirties and briefer hospitalizations, he managed his paranoid schizophrenia without medication.

*Manic episode: row Shearwater to Horn Island in the skiff, no matter the weather. Take food, a journal to record the days, pencils, paint. The skiff is home. Watch the animals. Stay until it passes.*

While he and his wife Agnes lived separately after 1945, they remained married until his death from lung cancer in 1965.

## II. ELIZABETH

[ - ]

This happens in the Carolinas, Chicago, Houston, on disappearing coasts, in a Mississippi I never was a part of.

Sometimes illness is a ghost that keeps up its haunting, even after you move states.

Not a love story for lushness. Neurons misfire but make good art. Not an elegy. Not a suit to stop an Elizabeth haunting an artist, long gone, wanting answers.

I draw a tree in chalk to signify the forest behind my home. I draw a body for the girl who was, before an illness. I draw a body for the Elizabeth who feigns politeness when it's necessary.

I'm ready at the board, eraser in hand.

## III. ILLNESS, A REVISION: WALTER

He knew exactly when the night bus would come charging down the overpass. It curved but never bled into the ditch.

Walter paints the progress of the day's light on the walls and ceiling of a room made quiet by his own longing.

He uses the fireplace to burn the work he does not want to live.

After his death, the fireplace is all ash.

## III. ILLNESS, A REVISION: ELIZABETH

One night, I see the man who knew my brain in every state, when I wanted him to. Now I'm a not-wife. I turn down another street.

The Brazos floods. I take medication. Look at MRIs (*with & without contrast*).

The river crests. Cows and cars float on an interstate in Pearland, their owners equally confused.

This isn't a dream or the rapture. This is Texas.

Who's to say how a body can revise.

✦

✦

# CONTENTS

# I.

*I heard a cry, how far away I couldn't tell . . .*

*before me—a Loon, . . . the strange hot eyes . . .*

—WALTER ANDERSON

✦

## HALF VILLAIN, HALF FOOL

When the delirium comes, I'll remind you not to run into windmills.
You won't listen. We are all waiting for some kind of rapture.


Let's take all our medications and put them in a swimming pool.
We'll do swan dives and still be safe, the drugs having kept us afloat.


Once madhouses held lunatic balls. Even the crazy look sane given
tempo.
Shuffle back to me. I'll put glitter in your ear and hold you like I'm
losing you.


Let's drive but keep our eyes on the roof. Don't turn right or left.
The car will run out of gas and save us from these crazy gods.


I'm only Elizabeth when I'm in trouble. You only love me when
I save you.
I'll be the owl and you the snake. We'll take turns consuming each
other.

## LET'S PRETEND

There's another way to be born. It's something
        to do with sea gulls as scavengers, hurricanes,

how the dunes rise up like breath and swallow me.
        It's something like building a ship. I'm

assembling my body with a typewriter so I can label
        all my bones: *Property of Walter I. Anderson.*

Someone puts me together incorrectly—
        *skull 1, vertebrae 2, sternum 3*—useless list.

You bandage my bruises. I eat the gauze.
        I can heal from the inside.

My typewriter-ribs begin to clack their own
        little story. They are rewriting me.

My typewriter-ribs are saying, *Let's leave again.*
        Sorry. I can't behave for you. Just

pretend there was another way
        for my mind to work. I'll even

let you play mad doctor. Take out what you think
        makes me walk into the ocean every night.

# ODE FOR AN ELIZABETH

Who could tell me about the twenty types of green found
on the coast of Pascagoula but a Walter, or an Elizabeth?


How I want a gator's four-chambered heart,
wishing, greedily, for three of them, how I'd use
those spare parts for all my desire.


A heart under the tongue, a heart twinning the hip,
heart inside the stomach, four-chambered,
two types of blood and like a marathoner,
running steady until it can't.


And when my heart skips a beat, I envision
it is trying to migrate within the body but knows
movement is casualty and stays put


but sullen. My needy heart mocks itself.
Don't talk to me of goldenrod or the tides.
Just dress for the hunt.

## IN WHICH RECALLING LOVE STORIES,
## WE WRITE A KINDER HISTORY

I took you to Oldfields—it rested there,
at the mouth of the Pascagoula. No view
could calm you like the ocean. I left
and back at college in Boston I skated
on the Charles, dated boys

who mumbled into soups. In summer,
there had been the red tide
of the sound. It was the summer

of meteor showers. I tried to teach you
about science and velocity
and jellyfish and their phosphorescence.
I was always the practical one.

And you wrote the word *bloom*
on a scrap of paper, buried it in the aloe plant I kept killing.
You could always coax dead things back.

## IN WHICH RECALLING LOVE STORIES,
## WE WRITE AN HONEST HISTORY

You steal your clay
from the Beaux Rivage, swearing
it smells like magnolias
even after firing.

I come to the studio
at Shearwater, watch you
at the wheel.

Clay never disappears—
it's between your hands,
being spun into a vase,
it's a mark on your neck,
a line of grit in the sink.

You push me to the floor
and all I think is:
I shouldn't wear linen.
It tears too easily.

I am clay in a pit fire.
To burnish is to blacken with luster.

If the wind is strong enough,
cool me. Paint me with a glaze.
Bind us.

# ESCAPE IS IN YOUR GENES

## I.

Delphine, my grandmother, began it all.
Knew rescue was never coming—

sewed gold coins into woolen hems,
drove her wagon New Orleans to Maryland.

Where the Potomac meets the Chesapeake
she saw men hanging by their thumbs,

others softening bones in a fire
for the marrow. Branches,

heavy with frost, snapped like shots.
She found her husband in *the boneyard*,

burying blue-lipped men. She lifted up
her dress, ignored the rats,

unwound clothes from her legs for him.
We all learn illusion early. She looked away

as he wept and changed and wept.

II.

I knew you couldn't be a constant
so I let the doctors guide you

to a room far from me. I knew you were
past help. When you escaped

from the hospital, your apology: a drawing of birds
in flight. Ivory soap and red brick

as good a canvas as any. Remember:
a group of black skimmers

is called a conspiracy. A kiss is birdlike impatience.
The radio in your mind tells you no one

is to be trusted, that I am made of potter's clay
so when you put your hand to my throat you are really

molding me, that you can swallow this plaster,
turn into a statue, spy on me.

III.

I cannot tie you to any place or any truth,
but I am tired of your tricks. So I have learned my own.

I learn of a man named John—
cabinetmaker by birth, maker of hidden things by God.

He built hiding places for priests during the reign of Henry,
breaking stone, at night, alone. Before beginning work, always

a prayer and then he'd take the host—*Lord I am not worthy*—
He built sliding doors, used illusion to fool the eye.

He was a trickster like you, escaping twice
from those hunting him, but finally in London's towers

they hung him by his wrists and even then
though they begged—*Only say the word*—he kept his secrets.

They say his bowels spilled from him. They say he died in peace.
I have learned to be a hidden thing you cannot break.

# II.

*Although Mr. Anderson has been with us for a year now,
I do not believe we are nearer a diagnosis . . . the real and
terrible qualities of this man's psychosis, and the trouble
he has been . . . this man is certainly the most difficult
we have had in years . . .*

—Dr. Louis Sharp, April 1938
The Phipps Clinic, Baltimore, MD

✦

# INDIANA, POST-HARVEST

When the fog comes off the fields, this is when
I miss you most. It lifts slowly, first revealing a line

of broken stalks, then an entire country of corn
past harvest. The silos are full and my father

is hiding in his office. If you were here,
we'd sit in the kitchen, I'd break up cornbread

into a glass, pour cream over it, show you
how this meal, at night's end, is both

sweet and filling. We'd make love in the back bedroom
and after, lie on our sides, look out the window

to the straight lines of fields. I'd ask you to tell me the story
of when you first loved me: how I climbed the silo's scaffolding

and you followed me because I told you I knew
this country, that I was a farmer's daughter.

You told me of a country where things are still done by hand,
of a home with thin fish, of places you can't reach

in the rainy season, and how if you still lived there,
you might leave for months but only because

*The river has swallowed the roads. I could not*
*come back to you, forgive me.* I would stop

taking pictures of power lines. Of fog.
I would put down the camera. Be there, ready,

when I heard the door slam.

# I DO NOT GO INTO THE DARK HOUSE

Heat, salt on the tongue,
a tumbler filling again.


In Charleston, mortar from brick
outlasts me. I run the battery and watch
what could be a funeral pyre drift on an ocean
known for lack of violence.


In Charleston, I run the battery.
The gulls don't follow me.
I have no gifts. I have enough
hair for a low braid.


Hours away, my brother
goes into a dark house.
I tell my mother
to watch his hands. I know
in the house he burns his fingertips
and finds a pyre.


We never speak.
I wonder if he kissed a cell
and the metal was our childhood
as we cracked pecans for our mother.

How he broke shells. I, tasked
with taking meat from offal.
In Charleston, I take the slur off my words,
get mistaken for Ohio. I rebuild myself genteel.

Brother, the deaths in Wagner are slaughter
not so far from the Carolinas.
Brünnhilde sleeps in a pyre.
We all live with flame. Who knew sadness
came in octaves?

I can't build a wall of sopranos or send it in a letter.

I don't write you. You would know
the house, or that at least
I've been making my own pyres.

# LET'S SAY A STORM IS A TYPE OF CONFESSION

You tell me the clouds are in the house again,
and when you wake in the night, tornadoes are
on the bedroom wall.

It has been a spring without rain.

You say you are the reason for this drought.
You cut your body     *it is the only way to make*
*the rains come back*     you say     *I have taken*
*in all the storms*     you say     *I am a dervish no*
*I am a tornado*     *I have taken up this house and*
*broken the china*     *I am*     *I am*     *I am—*

The tornadoes are heavy with the weight of
you.  You are spiraling. You are taking me
over.

You are *Turning again*, you say. You have been
jumping into the cold river. It is March. The
swallows are still gone. You cannot calm
yourself.
There is a scale to rate this devastation. Zero

bends a tree. A five rips buildings from their foundations.

There is nothing for us to do but get out anyway.

# WE WERE TWENTY AND LEAN AND HUNGRY

September's hunt: night, throwing lanterns

into the darkest corners.

Swamp smell: damp, sludge-thick,

trunks split open, dying in the water.

Everything grows slower here.

Pushing off the boat—no words

for the grass

catching shins, elbow, back of a throat.

Some pole during the day,

skimming the water to hook a gator

but night demands more.

Demands that you are calm,

that you breathe and follow the current.

Do not feed the baby gators.

They will lose their fear of us,

see the human

as a hand with food. A hand as food.

Instead, throw light

and wait for the red eye:

the one thing that betrays them.

I have seen gators grab a boar,

drag it down until it drowns.

Then the death roll:

snap of a jaw, wild spin

until head separates from body.

The blessing of dark water.

But beauty too:

the creature

sliding through the swamp.

Blending into tallow and fern.

# WE MAKE A HISTORY

With one hand you turn the pages
and with another sketch cities.
Why Beethoven? Why the concerto?
A small eye gleams.

Imagine to bury. To bury a dress
in the bottom of a box and vows,
lip balm, long hair, the knowledge
you will wake alone, for years.

A sail and a curtain of rain. How it all
descended. And in the night you will
say my name until it loses the body it belongs to.
And in the night a woman

sketches a dress back onto a body,
her hair into rows, scrubs away sadness.

## APOLOGY

No amount of prayer or balm can fix this.
Your body cannot find north.

It is entirely dark.

You are a sad twin, standing at the bed's edge,
counting your mistakes.

A man leaves, says you have a knife
where your heart should be.

This is why the compass won't obey you,
why the doctors can't find your pulse.

It is dark. Entirely.

# LEST YOU BECOME LUNATIC

Maryland snowstorm.          I escape in my hospital whites.

Mississippi is bankrupt.     Agony.          Pelicans, the mouth of
    the Davis Bayou,

    I swim out, find myself among them. Stay until they fly.


    When you ax the head off a fish,

it will sink like a stone into water. I set fire to *Missa solemnis.*

Newton's second law. The body that cannot change

    unless the swamp changes me. Can I burn and sink?

Will the pyre sail if my body has turned          animal?

A pulling of thread, tighter and tighter. Do not take your clothes
    off under the moon,

    lest you become lunatic.


Sleep to the bulrushes.

    Rise and move into the day's light.

# LOVE SONG, DIRGE, HALF APOLOGY

This is how I take my wife

for a walk in the dunes,

kill the lamplight, send her running

into night's dark mouth.

A bruised love,

rabbit in a low place, lean

and hungry creature. I could have

told you to walk east, given you

a night with a half-moon.

Some sort of path.

You say you are *cold*, wife.

What's hunted, tonight?

Death moves only one way. It is

to the bottom of this river. The air

is water. I close off your mouth. I am

a lifeguard saving you. I am coming

for your throat. I am sharpening my hands

for a creature that keeps changing.

# III.

*Until you can show me, in your letters, that
you have lost that dreadful willingness—even
pleasure—in remaining just as is, I cannot
give you false hope...I cannot live with you
in that state.*

—Agnes Anderson to Walter

✦

# HOW ALL THINGS ARE MANAGED

They call it a *Falling into death.*

Two dogs are shot into my vein.
Three-second breath then
the shake and jerk.
One dog starves and the other
feeds on its body.

Remember: Thou art dust.

If I am lucky, there is only the darkness,
an explosion.

Perhaps a fracture,
a concussion,
a dislocation.
Flecks of blood.

If the illness in your brain is brutal,
be brutal back.

# DESTRUCTION A HYMN I KEEP HUMMING

I.

An ache, a dismantling.

And at the window,

when you thought it went

from gloaming to darkness more quickly tonight,

it's because it did.       I walked through the woods,

pulling up what gives light.

Gullyful of ironweed. The S curve of a dove. Fence posts.

Your wife's heart.       Never frantic.


Once, I crawled into the low box of a grave

to best love my fear.       If a man loves me,

he loves shadow. Taste metal?

Thirsty?       Ignore this crowbar.

It is not for you.

We scavenge, Walter—

glass and canvas. The wind,

coming off the gulf tonight, calm.       Deny.

II.

Each day, I leave the woods, lie in the boat, turn to heat,

blister, beg, make the bones of the skiff

my own gentle coffin,

body inside a body, fever,

think of how to begin,

how to break your walk to shuffle.


The world is sleeping and I sit up in the skiff,

white flame in water. I row.

The killdeer are quiet, the crows mutter.

I go to Shearwater, tie the boat, walk the dock.


It is 1952, why would you lock the door?


I have paint, brushes, and a plan.

The first night, as you sleep upstairs,

I stand in your studio, take away animals.

I leave the red of the sun,

reeds, brackish water.

I take only what I think will make you stop—

a murmuration, fish gills, the coil of a snake.

III.


I cleaned up well.

Sure I wouldn't need a second night, I sang, Walter.

    I washed brushes in the kitchen sink,

paint down a drain, wondered if

families share the same night-breath, sang Nina Simone

and thought of smoke.


I slept on the ground at Shearwater—

Delta soil is soft enough for this—

and when I woke,

I watched the windows of your studio.


I waited.

    I wished you into being and there you were,

body at the edge of a room. You saw it,

my erasure. Hiccup of shoulders.

Then, back, paint in hand.

    I ground my teeth

and deer flies bit my shoulders

as you smiled, painted beasts back onto canvas.

You thought it play.

If the body a house,

the mouth a door,

the brain a basement,


I am unlocking things at the bottom of the stairs,

waiting for chaos in Mississippi.

IV.

I'm quick tonight. Anger makes me that way.
I take all things with ribs. All breath, hungry love,
the backs of cats, hook of a horse's neck.

Tonight, also, I take water, in every corner of your work.
I've grown deliberate. I take oyster shells.
Then the whole gulf—symphony and death rattle.

I take the Beaux Rivage, cypress, the ocean
as it unfurls and gulls skimming for meat,
gone too. I leave one suggestion of light. Here,

the shadow of a body at the door. Here the body
that was a marriage. Gravedigger at the ready.
Here the girl-not-a-girl taking all that moves, aches, bends,

disappears. Once I danced alone in kitchens. Who was I, then?

V.

I watch from the same spot. The reeds,
turning color: not reeds. Me. Again.

You pause. I see it. You set your jaw.
Pull easels, get frantic,
turn the water darker,
cypress-stained, paint rats in a corner,
caged things. A storm, breaking moon,
beach made bare.

June in Mississippi. How we learn
to love the heat, wait for dusk,
ride bicycles behind trucks billowing
mosquito repellent, not yet knowing
how poison sickens the body.

This is June. A sea leaving.

My dissolution.

VI.


Tonight, Shearwater is quiet but not still.
I walk into the studio. You,

twenty of you, landscape, portrait.
You, the shrill of night,

you, slip and mud and potter's wheel.
You, waist-deep in the gulf,

you, the shore, belonging. How I waited.
A shell, painted strangely, made iris.

Veins of an arm blazing star,
bird's wing, morphed: arch of a foot.

The spine of the body—gully.
The image, still wet to touch.

How you fret and breathe and challenge me.
I'm just a dark animal buried by night.

Destructive. I cannot give this up.

VII.

In the Atchafalaya Basin,

fathers teach sons the beauty of night-hunts—

stillness. They will become laconic men,

and perhaps this was my trouble. That I hunted

like a man, and spoke like one, meaning, never.

What's the trick, Walter? Will I ever be well?

I can't keep up the game. I take your canvas

and stand in the swamp. There was a gator.

I wonder what it ate first—the sky or your profile?

I could have stopped this.

Brought back your work for salvage.


What did we do before the moon

when there were things to dispose of?

I walked with a hymn in my mouth,

heel-striker that I am. And where moths

gather by the porch, and where your life

was built from light, I found you


in a room of empty frames. Detritus.

Didn't ask where they'd gone,

if I could bring them back.

Just a Pall Mall and marsh scent,

the dark mouth of night.

## PETER TO HIS BROTHER, ON THE STATE OF SHEARWATER

I made shapes to see them crack and blister. So sick of the trash and my daily failures, I took a hundred pieces and started a path between the marsh and deck.

I am looking for a glaze that recalls my wife as she walks the beach in winter. The year she spent in Paris, hours on the piano, and still she returned. I swear, when I kissed her neck, Chopin in the pulse.

Brother, you are in a Baltimore hospital and I am telling you, come home and see the family I have built in Mississippi.

The kiln is waiting for you, as are your brushes.

# I TEACH YOU TRANSPARENT THINGS

Yes, my father was a glassmaker. There is no worse punishment

than feeding the tin bath in summer. But I've gone too far.


First: learn to balance the equation. Sand and soda ash and lime, all
    added in approved

measurements and timings. Do not bring me beach sand, its faint
    scent of gulls and grass. It must


be from the vendor who delivers only on Tuesdays, his flatbed filled
    with 50-pound burlap bags. Sand and ash and lime:


the ash to dissolve and the lime so it will endure.

Cullet can speed the process but you must run it through your hands,


pull out the impure parts. If you aren't careful, the work will fail.

Other girls use windowpanes to check their image. I see process. I
    see before the window:


a furnace that runs five times hotter than an oven. Imagine a volcano,

ribbons of red lava. The furnace runs higher than that. Hotter than
    a volcano.


I wear the thinnest cotton but still I am an oil slick—

watching the clock, waiting for the fire to do its work. And after the
    furnace,

once things are molten, we open up the side door, let the spout lip
   pour out
ribbons of glass into the bath. Imagine pulling taffy.


Imagine it so flux you cannot
catch it. Imagine it spills onto the floor


but the floor has disappeared and you are standing in water, watching
   things solidify.
This is what it's like. Soon the glass will cool into sheets, still too
   hot for us to touch


so machine hands pull these squares, roll them into another machine.
   Cut them.


You are the girl who fixes broken things. You are the girl who looks
   at windshields,


knows if the fracture is from a rock, a branch that fell after the storm,
a hard skull that glanced off the glass after impact.

# EDUCATION

Because I never listened like the others, I went alone

to the caves of Les Eyzies. Caves are bowls

we used to live within. Hollow me out and fill me

with the things I should know instead of the wants

I always have. I wanted to lie down like the bison.

I wanted to be a rib of something bigger. I kept

touching the stone, touching those pictures, asking,

  *Qu'est ce? Qu'est ce? What is this?*

but what I meant was: *How do I become this?* Because once

people used bison bones to build homes.

And there must be a way to marry the human

and the other. If not by bone or ash, let me die by water.

Let me churn my legs to the ocean's floor,

let the sharks gut me.

# IV.

*My mind is a perfect mess. I can't think.*

—WALTER ANDERSON

✦

# LIKE A KINDNESS, LIKE AN INTERROGATION

Walter,

I'm writing a one-act play about my obsession.

> *(Two wood chairs. Later, a hatchet. One*
> *lamp behind the chair to stage left. The neck*
> *of the lamp stretches above your head.)*

This sadness          not       snarling, no

bluster. More of a wolf's fur, undercoat so dank

with sweat and night hope left years ago.

Walter,

         I was pretty once.        I had grace.

Walter,

         I'd write notes to myself. *This is the day*

*you should leave,* I'd say. *Remember how he*
                And I'd cut the paper into

quarters, hide them in different pockets.

Daffodil blazer. Slate work pants. A maroon

winter coat. Because while he was smart to

anger, he was never studied. Would never t

hink to take scraps and put them together.

Walter.

         I liked being a wife.

            Once, before I wed, my mother

showed me off to a friend as we waited for a

movie to start. Held up my left hand in hers—

*Married! Married! Getting married!*

*My saddest daughter, fixed!*

      Her friend on a bench watching us,
hair curled Southern-big.

      I knew I was all wrong
and didn't yet know how to emulsify vinegar.
I'd fix this.

                  I was loved.

# POST-RECOVERY, WALTER TEACHES ME ABOUT ILLNESS

Go to the drugstore. Put on a pair of glasses.
These glasses will teach you to be me. Realize
everyone is staring at you. Look at a box of crackers.
The side of it has directions on how to make them
stop staring. It involves a hand across a mouth
to keep out whispers. It involves an umbrella
but instead of keeping the rain off their face
men put the umbrella in front their eyes
so they see nothing as you walk past them. Realize everyone
can still see you through the umbrella-as-a-shield. Realize
the orange juice is poison. Drink nothing. Break
a thermometer and eat it. You are all the storms,
all the light. Break pencils and eat them. You are a pine.
You are a pine with termites, turning empty.
When the doctors x-ray you, see the pencil stamped
*Johns Hopkins Hospital.* Listen. The hum of the x-ray
is a murmur saying you'll always be *off*.
Eat more pencils.

## ASK TO HEAL, TO DROWN

I come early one day, find you wrapped
in wet sheets, mumbling, louder now,

cicada to loon, and I check your hands
to see if you're manic, if you're thrumming yet.

You're swallowing water again.
Making yourself a sea. You must stay dry.

If you're waterlogged, how can I keep
you close to me? You are seal-wet, ducking away,

childlike. Later, wound and gauze,
some ailment you keep wrapping, re-wrapping,

hours, your hand, you on the bed's edge,
eyes fixed on a sadness I can't see. Once,

you unwrapped this dress from me,
not once, often, and I too young to know

when you said, *There's something wrong in me*—
not a challenge but a warning.

# EXTINCTION

There is only one of me
the half-bird man
& the men are confused
because I was to die
ten years ago

they have graphs & a timetable
but I keep burning them
the papers they give to my wife
saying *Walter Anderson, dementia praecox*
*recurring delusions (self as bird—self as god—self*
*as father) catatonic / manic episodes*
these papers are a code
meaning *why is he still alive*
*this species no longer exists*
*make the anomaly*
*disappear*

Wings are inside my body
it's why I'm so itchy
truth in x-ray
sometimes I am a zoo
filled with angry mammals
it's why I mutter
& my heart beats fast
& I claw at you

my wings are grown together

stop calling them ribs

just give me a knife

I will show you

when I'm open


If I could

just get to my wings

I would have lift—

leave here


Please don't sigh & lock the windows

# WRECKAGE

New Order's on the radio, Perry Como's next,

I've got a green skiff lashed to the roof of this car.


I've got a paper hat that turns me into a demon

and by demon I mean I know you, Walter.


I am taking this car and coming to Shearwater.

I've got a 1952 Oldsmobile, lovingly restored,


and when I drive this car, each mile takes me

back a year so I'll get to you soon enough.


I am going through the belly of the swamp

and Walter, I've got white paint


and a need to make you cry.

The radio in your mind tells you


no one is to be trusted and when the clouds

roll in from the east the sky is a threat


as is anyone in your way, but if you paint

enough birds you can take flight.

Walter, pelicans are laying eggs too thin
to hatch and I'm grinding my teeth, waiting.

I'm not sweet. I'm not your wife. I wear red lipstick.

The first time, I failed. I sang the bruises
into healing. I waited, until you were ready

to invite me in. We paint over the canvas together.
We both find blankness.

# DEATH ROLL

Walter,

I drive the basin late at night

when the tank's on empty.

The sweetest word I know?—*Atchafalaya.*

How long before the engine seizes and I die here?

What language will I find when this one leaves me?

Walter, I begged a gator:

*Take me to the bottom of a lake.*

He opened one eye, as if to say,

*this isn't the romance I expected,* and he refused, Walter,

though I said, *Please,*

*please.* I had a monster ripening in me,

a lovely one, and it was stubborn in its loving.

I tried to make my ribs a skiff.

Sail away from my own heart. If I had more

than a spoon, I'd carve my body into territories,

leave all this on a trail overgrown with ferns.

Let another be queen of this body.

Gut me. Give me back.

This grief's window—

closing.

✦

# ACKNOWLEDGMENTS

Grateful acknowledgment is made to the publications in which these poems first appeared, sometimes in slightly different forms:

*Indiana Review:* "Extinction," "Indiana Post-Harvest"

*New South:* "We Were Twenty and Lean and Hungry," "Love Song, Dirge, Half Apology"

*Salt Hill:* "Let's Pretend"

*Tin House:* "How All Things Are Managed"

The deepest gratitude to my many teachers along the way, including a special thanks to Kevin Prufer for his generous editorial eye and spot-on comments on these poems. Thank you to Tony Hoagland, Martha Serpas, Marianne Boruch, Donald Platt, and Amy Quan Barry—your insight and mentorship over the years has been a wonderful gift.

For their generous friendship and feedback over the years, thank you to Janine Joseph, Caitlin Maling, Laura Donnelly, Jennifer Keplinger, Christina Martin, Dawn Gillespie, Brittany Duncan, Sara Cooper, Allyn West, Steve Sanders, Analicia Sotelo, Karyna McGlynn, Talia Mailman, J. Kastely, my Inprint and WITS families, Adrienne Perry, Dino Piacentini, Erika Jo Brown, Justine Post, and David Tomas Martinez.

Thank you to my friends and colleagues—too many to name—who have shown incredible kindness and support to me along the way.

Thank you to Christopher Maurer whose book, *Fortune's Favorite Child: The Uneasy Life of Walter Anderson*, provided invaluable research and served as the inspiration for this project.

For giving me the gift of time and space to work, thank you to the Creative Writing Program at the University of Houston, the Inprint organization of Houston, the I-Park Foundation, the Bread Loaf Writers' Conference, and the Vermont Studio Center.

Thank you the team at Alice James Books—they are a dream of a press, and their hard work made this book possible. A big thank you to Carey Salerno, Alyssa Neptune, and Matt Pennock for their help in shaping this work.

Thank you to my family for their unending support of me over the years. Most importantly, thank you to my parents, Mary Elaine and Joseph. Your belief in me is the brightest light.

# RECENT TITLES FROM ALICE JAMES BOOKS

ALICE JAMES BOOKS has been publishing poetry since 1973. The press was founded in Boston, Massachusetts as a cooperative wherein authors performed the day-to-day undertakings of the press. This collaborative element remains viable even today, as authors who publish with the press are also invited to become members of the editorial board and participate in editorial decisions at the press. The editorial board selects manuscripts for publication via the press's annual, national competition, the Alice James Award. Alice James Books seeks to support women writers and was named for Alice James, sister to William and Henry, whose extraordinary gift for writing went unrecognized during her lifetime.

*Designed by Dede Cummings*

*Printed by McNaughton & Gunn*